Photography and Belief

David Zwirner Books

ekphrasis

Photography and Belief
David Levi Strauss

[I am] forced to proceed like the materialist—that is, by observation and experience—and to conclude in the language of the believer, because there is no other.
—Pierre-Joseph Proudhon, *System of Economical Contradictions, or the Philosophy of Misery*, 1846, translated in 1888

If material conditions need to be redescribed, more painstakingly and in novel forms, in order to be reinvested with "believability," then we can surely develop the forms—and the means of dissemination—to do so.
—Martha Rosler, "Image Simulations, Computer Manipulations: Some Ethical Considerations," 1988

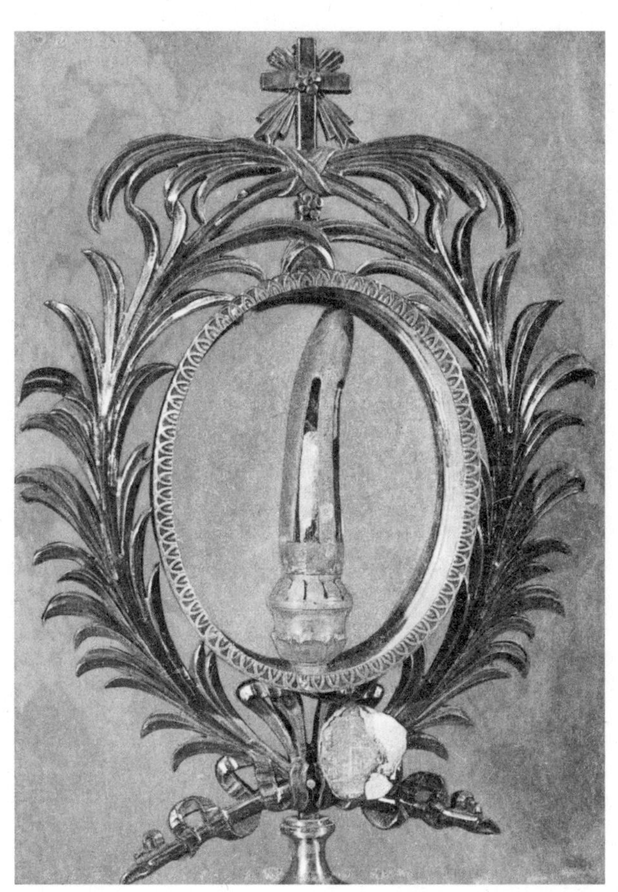

Contents

Chapter 1

> The symbolic order is assured as soon as there are images, in which one unfailingly believes, for belief itself is an image: the two sorts of image are constituted by the same processes and start with the same terms: memory, sight, and love or will. —Julia Kristeva[1]

Memory, because we remember primarily through images, and we believe what we remember (sometimes to our detriment); sight, because "Seeing is believing"; and love, because believing grows from the same root as loving.

Belief involves the acceptance of something as true. It comes from the strong agreement of the intellect, but the intervention of the will is always required to convince the intellect to agree.

The origin of the proverb "Seeing is believing" is lost in the mists of time. When it first appeared in print, it was already being quoted as an ancient saying. As Cervantes said, "A proverb is a short sentence based on long experience."

The year this proverb was first printed in English is usually given as 1609, in an unpublished manuscript by S. Harward (now housed in the library of Trinity College, Cambridge), where it emerges as "Seeing is leeving." *Leeving* is loving. The term comes from the Indo-European root *leubh*, meaning "to love or desire": the Anglo-Saxon *leof*, English *lief*, is "dear," "beloved." To believe is to hold dear. Believing is loving.[2]

Émile Benveniste, in his *Dictionary of Indo-European Concepts and Society* (1969), focuses on the Latin term *credo* (from *credere*, "to believe"), and its derivations, which extend the meaning of "credit" to include "belief." The connection of these two terms is ancient. Benveniste also focuses on the related word *kred*: "In the current view *kred* is regarded as a separate word signifying 'magic power'; *kred-dhe* thus signifies 'to put one's *kred* in somebody' (which results in trust)." Then Benveniste wryly notes, "This is not exactly simple but we cannot *a priori* expect such a notion to correspond to modern ideas."[3]

In his foreword to the 2016 edition of Benveniste's *Dictionary*, Giorgio Agamben points to a handwritten annotation to the great linguist's last lecture at the Collège de France that reads, "Language is not only *signalic* [informational,] … it is *nuntial* [enunciatory]." In other words (Agamben's), language "does not merely list signs in place of things, but proclaims or utters the *real*."[4] Perhaps this gesture toward the "phenomenology of the future" can now be applied to photographic images.

Blessed Are Those Who Have Not Seen

While seeing and believing have been joined together for a very long time, one of the most significant formulations of this union in the Judeo-Christian tradition focuses on its inverse. When Thomas doubts that Christ has risen from the dead, Jesus shows him his wounds from the crucifixion, and only then is Thomas convinced. But Jesus admonishes him, saying, "Have you believed because you have seen me? Blessed are those who have not seen and yet believe" (John 20:29).[5] This is really the opposite of "seeing is believing." It asserts that believing should not be dependent on seeing—that believing based on sight is an inferior belief.

Some see Thomas as an avatar of postmodern skepticism, uncertainty, and doubt, and as a harbinger of a future where we can no longer believe what we see. He had to be shown the wounds, as a therapeutic act, to know the trauma. And how can we not think here of the long history in photography of documenting trauma? Of the entire history of war photography, disaster photography, photojournalism, and social documentary? Of the forensic need to see in order to believe, to be able to feel "the pain of others" (as Susan Sontag put it in her last published book[6]), to understand the pain of the world (as John Berger wrote in his introduction to *Between the Eyes*[7]).

*

*   *

I like the word believe. In general, when one says "I know," one doesn't know, one believes. —Marcel Duchamp[8]

In his 2005 book *Doubting Thomas*, Glenn W. Most points out that what most people know (or think they know) about the story of Thomas—that he put his finger into the wound in Jesus's side—is not true. Or, at least, it's not biblical. It's not in the Gospels. But people believe it because they've seen it, over and over again, in numerous pictures.

In the twentieth chapter of the Gospel According to John, Mary Magdalene is the first to arrive at Jesus's tomb on the morning of the Resurrection. When she sees that the body of Jesus is no longer there, she runs to get Simon Peter and Thomas, the latter referred to here only as "the other disciple, the one whom Jesus loved" (some traditions believe John is "the other disciple"). When Thomas sees that Jesus is no longer there, "he saw and believed." In the evening, when Jesus comes to where the disciples are, Thomas is not there. Later, the other disciples tell Thomas what they have seen and heard, and he says, "Unless I see in his hands the print of the nails, and place my finger in the mark of the nails, and place my hand in his side, I will not believe."

Eight days later, Jesus again comes to where the disciples are, and this time Thomas is there. And Jesus says to Thomas, "Put your finger here, and see my hands; and put out your hand, and place it in my side; do not be faithless, but believing." And Thomas exclaims, "My Lord and my God!" And then Jesus says to him, "Have you believed because you have seen me? Blessed are those who have not seen and yet believe."

Thomas does not put his finger or hand into the wounds, because seeing them and hearing the risen Christ speak to him is enough.

Chapter 20 ends with these verses: "Now Jesus did many other signs in the presence of the disciples, which are not written in this book; but these are written that you may believe that Jesus is the Christ, the Son of God, and that believing you may have life in his name."

The belief in question here is one central to the Christian faith. If you do not believe in the Resurrection, if you do not believe that Jesus rose from the dead, you are not a Christian. And you must believe this on faith, not on the evidence of your (physical) senses. The "good news" of the Gospels is precisely this: Christ is risen. So, the stakes here couldn't be higher. As Paul says in 1 Corinthians 15:14, "If Christ has not been raised, then our preaching is in vain and your faith is in vain."

The entire discourse of doubt and conviction is centered on this one man, Thomas, the Twin. His name in Aramaic, T'ome, means "twin," and it is sometimes doubled, with the addition of the Greek *Didymos* (Διδυμοσ), meaning both "doubt" and "double." As Most puts it, chapter 20 of the Gospel According to John as a whole "can be read as an inquiry into the nature and limits of human belief and its relation to sensory knowledge."[9] Thomas is the representative of this relation, and the struggle to believe. As Augustine said, "He doubted that we might not doubt."

When John says, at the beginning of chapter 20, that Thomas "saw and believed," the original Greek (Jesus and the disciples spoke primarily in Aramaic, but the Gospels in their oldest form were written in Koine Greek) is *kai eiden kai episteuseu*. The verb is πιστευ, meaning to trust to or in, put faith in, rely on, to believe in a person or thing, to believe or give credit. This word for belief appears, in various forms, more than ninety times in the Gospel According to John. It appears only twenty-five times in all three books of the Synoptic Gospels (Matthew, Mark, and Luke).[10]

Even though the physical act of Thomas touching the wounds of Jesus does not occur in the Gospels, the image of it proved irresistible to artists. After his précis of the history of representations of doubting Thomas—from sarcophagi reliefs and ivory tablets from the fourth century to prints by Dürer, Schäufelein, and Schongauer, to paintings and sculptures by Caravaggio, Cima da Conegliano, Girolamo da Treviso, Mariotto di Nardo, Marco Pino, Rubens, Bernardo Strozzi, and Verrocchio, among others—Most writes:

> Thomas demanded not only to see Jesus, but also to touch him, if he was to believe. Viewers of these sacred images have only been able to see, and not touch, Thomas touching Jesus, yet many of them have believed because of these images that he really did.[11]

The Image of God

Theologians of Judaism, Christianity, and Islam have been examining the idea of the image of God for centuries. In the very first book of Moses, in Genesis 1:26, God said, "Let us make man in our image, after our likeness." And in Genesis 5:3, it is written that the first human, Adam, "became the father of a son in his own likeness, after his image." Martin Luther believed that "Man lost the image of God when he fell into sin."[12]

Fourth-century Christian theologians used the term "image" primarily as a Christological term. Christ, the Son of God, was an *image* of his father. The question of whether or not this "image" was distinct from the archetype, and therefore subordinate to it, was vexing to the early church. Colossians 1:15 portrays Jesus as a visible image of the invisible God. But rather than being subordinate, the image of Christ was presented as an eternal image through which all of God's creation springs into being: "All things were created through him, and for him" (Colossians 1:16). The Son is the active image that images all of the world, in heaven and earth, visible and invisible.

This question of the image of God (*Imago Dei*) is one of the instances in which we see Augustine's Platonism and Neoplatonism come into conflict with his Christian beliefs. To Plato, images are derivative (copies), and must always be seen as inferior to the true, original Forms. Augustine thought that humanity is located in the human mind, and so the image of God must be located there as well, in the trinity of memory, intellect, and will. In the twentieth century, Paul Ricoeur asserted that the image of God is actually free will.[13]

In her "Ellipsis on Terror and the Specular Seduction," Julia Kristeva notes,

> For St. Augustine, however deformed or vitiated an image may be, from the moment that it *is*, it supports the transcendental quest, even and perhaps all the more so if it is not the image of an identifiable object. Knowing this permits him that marvelous gesture of inverting Scripture: "Surely every man walketh in a *vain show* [=*image*]: surely they are disquieted in vain: he heapeth up riches, and knoweth not who shall gather them" (Psalm 39:6). For these lines St. Augustine substitutes the following: "Even though man be disquieted in vain, surely he walketh in the image."[14]

Walking in the image has always had a political as well as a religious import. The conflict between these two aspects—religious faith and political power—has swirled around images from the beginning of time, and continues to this day.

The First Photograph

My favorite branch of Turin Shroud literature is that which seeks to prove that the shroud is, in fact, a photograph—perhaps the first photograph ever made, in the thirteenth or fourteenth century. This "proto-photography" theory was perhaps most ingeniously argued by the art historian Nicholas Allen, in his PhD dissertation for the Department of Fine Arts at the University of Durban-Westville, in 1993, titled "The Methods and Techniques Employed in the Manufacture of the Shroud of Turin." A further twist on the proto-photography theory, put forth by Lynn Picknett and Clive Prince in their book *Turin Shroud*, published in 1994, is that this first photograph, made 350 years before the previously accepted advent of photography, in the 1820s, was made not by some anonymous medieval artisan but by none other than Leonardo da Vinci![15]

The Shroud of Turin has long been at the center of age-old battles about authenticity, iconoclasm, and belief in images. Many devout Christians around the world believe that it was the actual winding-sheet that Jesus Christ left behind in the cave when he rose from the dead (as recounted in the Gospels), and that its very existence is tangible proof of that event. Believers claim that the shroud is *acheiropoetic*; that, like the Veronica and the Mandylion, it is a direct emanation of the Son of God, unmediated, without human intervention or subjectivity: an objective trace. They believe that this image of the body of the crucified Christ, with all his wounds in evidence, was miraculously imprinted on this linen burial cloth at the time of Christ's Resurrection. That belief was shaken, but not broken, in October 1988, when carbon dating methods showed that the cloth did not date from the time of Christ but from much later, sometime between AD 1260 and 1390.

But long before the 1980s, photography played a significant role in shroud studies. In 1898, a lawyer and amateur photographer from Turin named Secondo Pia was allowed to take photographs of the shroud. When the negative image on the cloth was printed as a positive, the body and face depicted came alive. The photographs also made it possible for many more people to see the relic, and its influence spread. Its cultural presence took another big turn in 1973, when the shroud was exhibited on live television. In 1978, Ian Wilson's book *The Shroud of Turin* became a runaway best seller. In 2013, images of the shroud were streamed on various websites and are now, of course, available everywhere on the internet.

In recent years, the Catholic Church has been very careful about asserting the authenticity of the shroud. In a remarkably labyrinthine address on May 24, 1998, standing before the shroud in Turin, Pope John Paul II called it "one of the most unsettling signs of the Redeemer's suffering love," and "the precious linen that can help us better to understand the mystery of the love of God's son for us," but he also called it "a challenge to our intelligence." On questions about its authenticity, the pope demurred:

Since it is not a matter of faith, the Church has no specific competence to pronounce on these questions. She entrusts to scientists the task of continuing to investigate, so that satisfactory answers may be found to the questions connected with this sheet, which, *according to tradition*, wrapped the body of our Redeemer after He had been taken down from the cross. The Church urges that the Shroud be studied without pre-established positions that take for granted results that are not such: she invites them to act with interior freedom and attentive respect for both scientific methodology and the sensibilities of believers.[16]

Nicholas Allen (now at Nelson Mandela University, in Port Elizabeth, South Africa) assiduously avoids theological questions about the shroud in his dissertation, concentrating instead on the possibility of this artifact having been made in the medieval period using photographic techniques. As he says, if he proves this true, "it would necessitate a complete reappraisal of the history of photography as we know it."[17]

After recounting the history of interpretations of the shroud, from the first recorded account in 1357 to the present, and refuting each theory of its origin, Allen concludes that "this image could only have been produced by employing a photographically related technique." He then demonstrates that all the constituents of a photographically based technique—the workings of the camera obscura, light-sensitive chemicals (silver chloride and silver nitrate), and lenses—were known before 1260 and conceivably could have been combined.

A good deal of this knowledge came from the *Kitāb al-manāzir* (Book of Optics) of Ibn al-Haytham, an Arabic natural philosopher known in the Latin West as Alhazen, who lived from about AD 965 to about 1039. The seven volumes of the *Kitāb al-manāzir* contain extensive knowledge of optics, including the camera obscura (the Latin term was not coined until 1604, by Johannes Kepler, who also first used the term "camera" on its own for his portable version), and existed in Latin translations from 1250 on. Allen provides a similar précis of the medieval knowledge of light-sensitive reagents and lenses, and adds that there are certainly other historical examples of knowledge existing and then being lost for a period of time. Allen concludes his treatise by relating how he employed medieval methods to reproduce the image of the Shroud of Turin.

Why did it take so long to "invent" photography? The question has certainly been asked for a long time. So, it is irresistible to ask the follow-up question: What if it didn't take so long?

Picknett and Prince set out the theory that Leonardo made the shroud using a sixty- to one-hundred-year-old piece of cloth and proto-photographic techniques to produce a believable image of the body of the crucified Christ, to replace the inferior images in previous attempts at a Holy Shroud. They further posit that the image of the face on the Shroud of Turin, which has become one of the most iconic prototypes for the image of Christ, is in fact a self-portrait of Leonardo himself.[18]

It is not so much of a stretch to imagine that the Renaissance inventor of flying machines, submarines, armored vehicles, diving suits, and contact lenses might also have invented a kind of photograph. We know that Leonardo was fascinated with light and optics. We also know that he dissected cadavers to learn more about human anatomy, and focused specifically on the anatomical effects of crucifixion (even though he never painted a Crucifixion scene). He dissected a human eye and experimented extensively with lenses and mirrors and a camera obscura (he called it an *oculus artificialis*, or "artificial eye"). He even invented a light meter! If anyone could have found a way to fix an image of a body cast through an aperture or lens in a black box onto a sensitive emulsion, 350 years before the first photograph was known, it was probably Leonardo. And only Leonardo would have had the audacity to do it, as a hoax on (or by) the Church.

Picknett and Prince recognize what this would have meant at the time:

Today we are so familiar with the whole idea of photography that it is almost impossible for us to put ourselves in the place of someone encountering it for the first time. To the average Renaissance Italian, the act of capturing an image from life would have been regarded as a totally magical act. Try convincing the Church, which was highly suspicious of any innovation, that this was a perfectly natural process. . . . It is a fact that during the Middle Ages and Renaissance experiments with optics and light were kept strictly secret, and were firmly in the province of the magical adept.[19]

So, perhaps Leonardo accepted the commission, made the "relic," and kept it secret. This is their theory. Shroud literature is every bit as conspiratorially arcane as JFK-assassination literature, which is also centered on photographic evidence, especially the Zapruder film.[20] But both of these groups of literature—the sacred and the secular (religious faith and political power)—reveal much about the nature of image and belief.

Obviously, Leonardo wasn't the only one, or the first one, who dreamed of photography before the nineteenth century. Picknett and Prince point to a number of constitutive events in the prehistory of photography, including Aristotle's description of the camera obscura in the fourth century BC; the Roman poet Statius's description of capturing people's images on silver mirrors in his first-century AD works; and Pliny's mention of the light sensitivity of silver chloride in his *Natural History*, also in the first century; all the way up to the Hermeticist and alchemist Giovanni Battista della Porta's description of the camera obscura in 1552, and the Hermeticist and alchemist Athanasius Kircher's magic lanterns in the 1640s. Photochemistry arose from the work of alchemists with silver salts and many other light-sensitive materials, both organic and inorganic, at least as early as the twelfth century.

It might be said that by the time Nicéphore Niépce, Louis Daguerre, and William Henry Fox Talbot made their breakthrough technical discoveries in the nineteenth century, belief in photography had already been around for millennia.

Chapter 2

> There is a tender empiricism that makes itself utterly identical with the object, thereby becoming true theory. —Goethe

Walter Benjamin's most extended statement on photography, "Small History of Photography," appeared in three installments of the literary review *Die literarische Welt*, in September and October of 1931. Benjamin told Gershom Scholem that this piece "developed from prolegomena" to his *Arcades Project*.[1] His fascination with the new medium had been reawakened by his friendship with László Moholy-Nagy, whose book *Malerei Fotografie Film* (Painting Photography Film) was published in 1925, as well as by his friendships with the photographers Sasha Stone, Gisèle Freund, and Germaine Krull. In "Small History of Photography," Benjamin seeks to address "philosophical questions that attend the rise and decline of photography" that he thought hadn't yet been adequately considered.

When the piece appeared in 1931, it had virtually no impact on the photography world and was summarily ignored by nearly everyone else. In fact, it really didn't have any effect at all until the student revolts of the 1960s in Europe, after it was republished in Germany, in 1963, in a slim volume along with Benjamin's "The Work of Art in the Age of Technological Reproducibility" (1935–1938). "Small History" was finally published in an English translation in the 1970s (including in *Artforum* in 1977), just in time to have a considerable influence on post-modern photography and theory.

At the beginning of "Small History," Benjamin deftly rehearses the early history of the medium and says that this history of photography made it difficult "to develop genuine insights into its essence":

> The attempts to master the matter theoretically have been extremely rudimentary. And however much it was discussed in the last century, fundamentally there was never any abandonment of that laughable formula with which a chauvinistic rag, the *Leipzig Anzeiger*, thought it had to counter the French art of the Devil right from the start. "Wanting to fix fleeting reflections," it opines, "this is not merely an impossible quest, as thorough German investigations have established, but the very wish to do so is blasphemous. The human is created in the image of God and God's image cannot be captured by any man-made machine." ... This is how the philistine notion of "art" enters the stage, with heavyweight gaucheness.... It was this fetishistic, fundamentally anti-technical concept of art that the theorists of photography argued about for almost a hundred years, without, of course, getting anywhere at all.[2]

Benjamin saw something much more fascinating in photography, including an "optical unconscious," that he says one could only learn of through photography. "It is indeed a different nature that speaks to the camera than that which speaks to the eye," he writes, "different above all in the sense that a space saturated by a person who is conscious is superseded by one saturated unconsciously." He thought "the composition of structures, cellular tissue, all that stuff with which technology and medicine reckon to deal," were all primarily related to the camera:

> But at the same time, photography discloses in this material physiognomic aspects, image worlds, which inhabit the smallest things, interpretable and latent enough to have found a bolthole in daydreams. But now, as they have become enlarged and articulable, they make manifest how *the difference between technology and magic is a thoroughly historical variable*.[3]

We will return to the subject of technology and magic later. But, first, in "Small History," Benjamin gives one definition of "the aura," as "a peculiar weave of space and time: the singular appearance only of distance, however close it may be."[4] And this leads him to characterize our current and future relation to the photographic image: "Every day and more and more irrefutably the need asserts itself to grab hold of the object up close in an image, or rather a reproduction."[5]

Benjamin thought that early surrealist photography "cleared the way for a politically schooled gaze, according to which all intimacies abate in favor of the illumination of details."[6] This attraction to details, stripped of aura and intimacies, signaled a shift to a blasphemous belief in the thing itself.

Berger on Photography and Belief

The English translation of "Small History of Photography" that had the most reach early on was the one by Edmund Jephcott and Kingsley Shorter, included in the collection *One-Way Street and Other Writings*, published by Harcourt Brace Jovanovich in New York in 1978, and in London a year later by New Left Books, with an introduction by Susan Sontag. Another significant and revelatory theory of photography soon followed in John Berger's essay "Appearances," published in 1982 as part of his book with the photographer Jean Mohr, *Another Way of Telling*.[7]

Berger's essay arose from the experience of collaborating with his friend Mohr on the books *A Fortunate Man: The Story of a Country Doctor* (1967) and *A Seventh Man: Migrant Workers in Europe* (1975), during which both Mohr and Berger began to question a number of "the assumptions usually made about photography," concerning its objectivity and truth value. These assumptions accrued to photography from its historical context. When the first practical (daguerreotype) camera was introduced to the public in 1839, Berger points out, Auguste Comte was just completing his *Cours de Philosophie Positive*, which posits that the highest form of knowledge (greater than that of theology or metaphysics) is the simple description of sensory phenomena, based entirely on direct observation.

> Positivism and the camera and sociology grew up together. What sustained them all as practices was the belief that observable quantifiable facts, recorded by scientists and experts, would one day offer man such a total knowledge about nature and society that he would be able to order them both. Precision would replace metaphysics, planning would resolve social conflicts, truth would replace subjectivity, and all that was dark and hidden in the soul would be illuminated by empirical knowledge.[8]

This positivist utopia didn't quite occur, even though unprecedented scientific and technological progress did. What happened instead, in Berger's terms, was "the global system of late capitalism wherein all that exists becomes quantifiable—not simply because it *can be* reduced to a statistical fact, but also because it *has been* reduced to a commodity."[9] This transformation leads to a "primary suppression of the social function of subjectivity," which in turn affects both the uses of photography and its reception:

> Photographs, it is said, tell the truth. From this simplification, which reduces the truth to the instantaneous, it follows that what a photograph tells

about a door or a volcano belongs to the same order of truth as what it tells about a man weeping or a woman's body.

If no theoretical distinction has been made between the photograph as scientific evidence and the photograph as a means of communication, *this has been not so much an oversight as a proposal.*

The proposal was (and is) that when something is visible, it is a fact, and that facts contain the only truth.[10]

For Berger, then, at least as regards the public use of photography (as opposed to its individual, personal use), "the denial of the innate ambiguity of the photograph is closely connected with the denial of the social function of subjectivity."[11] Berger draws the distinction between appearances (what the eye sees) and what the camera records. As he says, "Photographs do not translate from appearances. They quote from them."[12] And this influences photography's relationship to truth. "In itself, the photograph cannot lie, but, by the same token, it cannot tell the truth; or rather, the truth it does tell, the truth it can by itself defend, is a limited one."[13] He asks if it is possible that appearances themselves constitute a language, since they do cohere and they do "possess some of the qualities of a code."[14] Eventually, he writes that appearances constitute a "half-language":

The half-language of appearances continually arouses an expectation of further meaning. We seek revelation with our eyes. In life this expectation is only rarely met. Photography confirms this expectation and confirms it in a way which can be shared. . . . In the expressive photograph, appearances cease to be oracular and become elucidatory. It is this confirmation which moves us.

Apart from the event photographed, apart from the lucidity of the idea, we are moved by the photograph's fulfillment of an expectation which is intrinsic to the will to look. The camera completes the half-language of appearances and articulates an unmistakable meaning. When this happens we suddenly find ourselves at home amongst appearances, as we are at home in our mother tongue.[15]

Berger's recognition of the "suppression of the social function of subjectivity" that arises from the denial of the innate ambiguity in photographs leads him to insights into the relation of photography and belief. The photographic surface, now confined mostly to screens, fleetingly completes the "half-language" of appearances but is also continually combined with words over time to activate belief, through memory.

Berger writes passionately about the violence done to the subjective experience by history, and about the concerted efforts by human beings to preserve experience in the face of this violence, as "hundreds of millions of photographs, fragile images, often carried next to the heart or placed by the side of the bed are used to refer to that which historical time has no right to destroy."[16]

Barthes on Photography and Belief

In *Camera Lucida* (1981), Roland Barthes sets out "to learn at all costs what Photography was 'in itself,' by what essential feature it was to be distinguished from the community of images."[17] The photograph, Barthes writes, points a finger at something and says, "Look, there it is." It "cannot escape this pure deictic language." What's more, this direct connection to the referent cannot be altered. As Barthes puts it, "the referent adheres." This is what makes it so hard to see photography for what it is, to consider the photograph itself, because of this inherent deflection. The world comes rushing in.

So, Barthes decides to focus on only a few photographs that are personally meaningful to him, to "make myself the measure of photographic 'knowledge.'" He asks, "What does my body know of Photography?" and the answer comes quickly, "that rather terrible thing which is there in every photograph: the return of the dead."

Barthes's approach, in the beginning, is generally phenomenological (the book is an homage to Sartre's phenomenology of the imagination), but he admits that it is "a vague, casual, even cynical phenomenology, so readily did it agree to distort or to evade its principles according to the whim of my analysis." What was inadequate about the classical phenomenology of Barthes's adolescence was that it "had never, so far as I could remember, spoken of desire or mourning." It could not, in other words, deal with *belief*. As a spectator, Barthes wanted to explore photography "not as a question (a theme) but as a wound." Like Thomas.

For Barthes's spectator, the *studium* is "a kind of general, enthusiastic commitment" that is cultural, and the *punctum*, which disturbs the studium, is a wounding, as pricks or points. The studium is "of the order of *liking*, not of *loving*," and under its terms, "it is rather as if I had to read the Photographer's myths in the Photograph, fraternizing with them but not quite believing in them."

Through what he calls the Winter Garden Photograph, an image of his recently deceased mother as a child, Barthes finds his way, where he must "interrogate the evidence of Photography, not from the viewpoint of pleasure, but in relation to what we romantically call love and death." The essence of photography is the certain belief that its referent had really existed, the "that-has-been":

> Photography has something to do with resurrection: might we not say of it what the Byzantines said of the image of Christ which impregnated St. Veronica's napkin: that it was not made by the hand of man, *acheiropoietos*?[18]

Barthes thinks the "that-has-been" or "intractability" of photography is something new in the world.

Perhaps we have an invincible resistance to believing in the past, in History, except in the form of myth. The Photograph, for the first time, puts an end to this resistance: henceforth, the past is as certain as the present, what we see on paper is as certain as what we touch. It is the advent of the Photograph—and not, as has been said, of the cinema—which divides the history of the world.[19]

And this new thing has a particular nature. "The realists, of whom I am one ... do not take the photograph for a 'copy' of reality, but for an emanation of *past reality*: a *magic*, not an art."[20] This kind of photograph "accomplishes the unheard-of identification of reality ('that-has-been') with truth ('there-she-is!'); it becomes at once evidential and exclamative."

At the end of his book, Barthes reflects on the current situation, politically. "What characterizes the so-called advanced societies is that they today consume images and no longer, like those of the past, beliefs; they are therefore more liberal, less fanatical, but also more 'false' (less 'authentic')." For Barthes, the choice is between mad or tame photography:

Tame if its realism remains relative, tempered by aesthetic or empirical habits ... ; mad if this realism is absolute and, so to speak, original, obliging the loving and terrified consciousness to return to the very letter of Time: a strictly revulsive movement which reverses the course of the thing, and which I shall call, in conclusion, the photographic *ecstasy*.

Such are the two ways of the Photograph. The choice is mine: to subject its spectacle to the civilized code of perfect illusions, or to confront in it the wakening of intractable reality.[21]

In *Camera Lucida*, Barthes tries to account for the hold a cherished photograph of his mother has over him, not so much due to its symbolic meaning (the studium), but in its personal, piercing meaning (the punctum). It is in the latter realm where belief comes in, following this wounding of desire and mourning, linked inexorably with the death and loss of the beloved.

Analogies

In the first volume of her history of photography, *The Miracle of Analogy* (2015), Kaja Silverman moves aggressively against "the notion that a photograph is a trace of its referent—and therefore both evidentiary and memorial," on the way to proving that "the photographic image is an analogy, rather than a representation or an index." To do this, she gives a fresh reading of the history of photography, beginning with the camera obscura ("From the late 1500s to the end of the 1700s … the camera obscura was perceived as a knowledge machine—a device for determining what was 'objectively true.'"[22]), and proceeding to the inventors Daguerre ("The DAGUERREOTYPE is not merely an instrument which serves to draw Nature; on the contrary it is a chemical and physical process which gives her the power to reproduce herself."[23]) and Fox Talbot ("It is not the artist who makes the picture, but the picture which makes *itself*."[24]).

> Photography isn't a medium that was invented by three or four men in the 1820s and 1830s, that was improved in numerous ways over the following century, and that has now been replaced by computational images. It is, rather, the world's primary way of revealing itself to us—of demonstrating that it exists, and that it will forever exceed us. Photography is also an ontological calling card: it helps us to see that each of us is a node in a vast constellation of analogies.[25]

Silverman is partly, one imagines, responding to Barthes, who writes:

> Nothing can prevent the photograph from being analogical; but at the same time, Photography's *noeme* has nothing to do with analogy (a feature it shares with all kinds of representations). . . . To ask whether a photograph is analogical or coded is not a good means of analysis. The important thing is that the photograph possesses an evidential force, and that its testimony bears not on the object but on time. From a phenomenological viewpoint, in the Photograph, the power of authentication exceeds the power of representation.[26]

Beyond the Index

As Franz Kafka told the young Gustav Janouch, "Nothing can be so deceiving as a photograph."[27] Nothing can be so deceiving because nothing promises truthfulness like a photograph. It is this promise of fidelity, of a special relation to the real, that makes the deceit so encompassing. Benjamin, Berger, and Barthes all analyze the promise of fidelity in photography in different but related ways.

One of the main bases for the truth claims of photography over the past forty years or so has been its *indexicality*. The term is drawn from Charles Sanders Peirce's semiotic theory of the three ways a sign may stand for its object: an existential connection (indexical), a likeness to it (iconic), or according to a habit or law (symbolic). Tom Gunning has made one of the most cogent arguments against the overreliance on indexicality when thinking about photography, in an essay titled "What's the Point of an Index? or, Faking Photographs," delivered to a colloquium on "Digital Aesthetics" and published in 2004.[28] "The apparatus, in itself," he writes, "can neither lie, nor tell the truth. Bereft of language, a photograph relies on people to say things about it or for it." Gunning argues, along with André Bazin in "The Ontology of the Photographic Image," that "a photograph puts us in the presence of something, that it possesses an ontology rather than a semiotics":

There is no question of mistaking a photograph for the world; its stillness, borders, sense of texture, etc., forbid that. Photography therefore does not affect me like a hallucination. But outside of some form of analysis, I am not sure we ordinarily approach photography semiotically, that is, taking them as signs. Certainly a photograph can function as a sign for something, usually its subject, a souvenir of a place or a person, a way of identifying or referring to something. But I think this is a secondary process to its ability as a picture to present us with an image of the world. … Whereas signs reduce their reference to a signification, I would claim the photograph opens up a passageway to its subject, not as a signification but as a world, multiple and complex.[29]

Gunning asks, "Is the indexical relation to a referent enough to truly explain what Bazin describes as photography's 'irrational power to bear away our faith'?" and answers in the negative:

I would claim that we still have only the beginnings of an account of the fascination photography exerts and although the use of the term "index" may have helped explain some aspects of this fascination, I am not at all sure it is either an adequate or accurate term. The semiotic category of the index assimilates photography to the realm of the sign, and although a photograph like most anything (everything?) can be used as a sign, I think this approach prematurely cuts off the claims made by theorists like Barthes, Bazin (and I think Deleuze) that the photograph exceeds the functions of a sign and that this indeed is part of the fascination it offers. . . . Here our delight in visual illusion may play as important a role as indexicality. And if we are to deal with illusions it seems to me that the play with photographic imagery that the digital revolution allows may provide the perfect playground/laboratory for a greater understanding of a fascination that I maintain is likely to have a future.[30]

Indexicality has served, over the past forty years or so, as a kind of materialization of belief.

Most of the truth claims for photography rely on various assertions of photography's "objectivity." In many of the earlier formulations, photographs were thought to be more objective than traditional images, without the human stain of subjectivity. This particular idea about photographs set up the long, involved struggle of photography to be accepted as art.

Benjamin, Berger, and Barthes all focused on the subjectivity of photography, especially its "social subjectivity." Their arguments for the subjectivity of photography become even more important as we move into the expanded realm of Vilém Flusser's "technical images."

Chapter 3

Flusser's Belief

Vilém Flusser's *Towards a Philosophy of Photography* was first published in German as *Für eine Philosophie der Fotografie*, by European Photography, in 1983, and later in Flusser's own English translation, in 1984, but it did not reach a wider Anglophone readership until Reaktion Books in London published Anthony Mathews's translation in 2000. It has since been translated into many languages all over the world.

Flusser's title is deceptively modest. *Towards a Philosophy of Photography* is an original phenomenological approach to photography, but it also introduces a radical theory about future sweeping changes in our communications environment that Flusser would continue to elaborate and interrogate until his untimely death in 1991 in an auto accident. He begins the book by stating the stakes involved with these coming changes:

> This book is based on the hypothesis that two fundamental turning points can be observed in human culture since its inception. The first, around the middle of the second millennium BC, can be summed up under the heading "the invention of linear writing"; the second, the one we are currently experiencing, could be called "the invention of technical images." ... This hypothesis contains the suspicion that the structure of culture—and therefore existence itself—is undergoing a fundamental change.[1]

In *Towards a Philosophy of Photography*, Flusser positions photographs as the first "technical images," and the camera as the first apparatus of the coming digital revolution, the first black box (the Portuguese version of the book published in Brazil is titled *Filosofia da Caixa Preta* [Philosophy of the Black Box]).

Like any good phenomenologist, Flusser begins by defining terms, and they are laid out in a "Lexicon of Basic Concepts" at the end of the book. *Image* is "a significant surface on which the elements of the image act in a magic fashion towards one another." *Magic* is "a form of existence corresponding to the eternal recurrence of the same." *Imagination* is "the specific ability to produce and to decode images." He contrasts the world of magic, "a world in which everything is repeated and in which everything participates in a significant context," with the world of history, "in which nothing is repeated and in which everything has causes and will have consequences," and concludes that "the significance of images is magical."[2]

Linear writing, Flusser contends, was invented in order to subdue the magical world of images with history, which begins "as a struggle against idolatry." "Texts do not signify the world; they signify the images they tear up," he writes. In the dialectic between texts and images, "textolatry reached a critical level in the nineteenth century," and history, per se, came to an end. "During this crisis of texts, technical images were invented: in order to make texts comprehensible again, to put them under a magic spell—to overcome the crisis of history."[3]

These technical images (initially, photographs and films, and eventually including television, satellite and computer images, holograms, and virtual reality) were very different, historically and ontologically, from traditional images (paintings and drawings) in that "traditional images signify phenomena whereas technical images signify concepts." Flusser points to the ontological status of technical images that makes them difficult to decode: "They appear to be on the same level of reality as their significance." Consequently, "their criticism is not an analysis of their production, but an analysis of the world," which makes it difficult to keep it within bounds as criticism. He warns, "This lack of criticism of technical images is potentially dangerous at a time when technical images are in the process of displacing texts—dangerous for the reason that the 'objectivity' of technical images is an illusion." Again, the stakes are high:

> The universe of technical images, emerging all around us, represents the fulfillment of the ages, in which action and agony go endlessly round in circles. Only from this apocalyptic perspective, it seems, does the problem of photography assume the importance it deserves.[4]

Flusser then embarks on an analysis of the camera as a black box, as the prototype of the ubiquitous apparatuses that are to come in the telematic world (an information society based on images). One way that these new apparatuses are different from the machines of the industrial world is that they do not intend to change the world, but "to change the meaning of the world. Their intention is symbolic."[5] In political terms, it is those who control the "soft programs," not the hard objects, who now have power: "This shift of power from the material to the symbolic is what characterizes what we call the 'information society' and 'post-industrial imperialism.'"[6]

In Flusser's reformulation, the camera has a program (in the sense of a computer program: a list of instructions telling the device what to do), and most humans taking photographs are simply functionaries in the service of this program. Thus, "their actions are automatic camera functions,"[7] and a kind of "ritual act" that produces "a permanent flow of unconsciously created images." In terms of reception, most people think that photographic images do not need to be decoded, since their relation to the real is self-evident. This makes it possible for humans to be persuaded and controlled by images, and to "act in a ritual fashion in the service of a feedback mechanism for the benefit of cameras."[8] It also makes a real criticism of photography extremely difficult.

The only way for photographers to make improbable images (to produce information) is to work against the camera's program. "This specifically human and at the same time unnatural ability is called 'mind,' and culture is its result, i.e., improbably formed, informed objects."[9] Or, what may be called art. Flusser believed that artists create reality. They have the ability to stretch the limits of language and create new forms.

Toward the end of his book, Flusser elaborates a dark vision of the programmed world to come. He defines the program as "a combination game based on chance," like the throw of dice: "In this subhumanly mindless sense, apparatuses 'think' by means of chance combinations. In this sense they are omniscient and omnipotent in their universes." In this way, human beings become pieces in the game, or functionaries: "The photographic universe and all apparatus-based universes robotize the human being and society."[10] Flusser calls for a new cultural criticism, to analyze this new order, and predicts that "within such cultural criticism, the camera will prove to be the ancestor of all those apparatuses that are in the process of robotizing all aspects of our lives, from one's most public acts to one's innermost thoughts, feelings, and desires."[11] He recognizes that the whole complex of apparatuses, beginning with photography, "is being linked up by cybernetics to other apparatuses," resulting in "a super-black-box made up of black boxes." What needs to be criticized and analyzed, he says, is the *automaticity* of apparatuses: "The criticism of apparatuses proposed here sees its task precisely in uncovering the terrible fact of this unintentional, rigid, and uncontrollable functionality of apparatuses, in order to get a hold over them."[12]

As in all of Flusser's writings, the principal concern, in the end, is human freedom. But how does this apply in the future of technical images, when life will mean "feeding apparatuses and being fed by them"? In the last section of *Towards a Philosophy of Photography*, Flusser asks the question, "If everything is based on chance and necessarily results in nothing, then where is there space for human freedom?" His answer is to look to the photographers he points to earlier, who are working against the program of the camera and producing improbable images (he calls them "experimental photographers"). Flusser doesn't give any examples of these, but I would think here of artists including Chris Marker, Jean-Luc Godard, Robert Frank, Harun Farocki, Joan Fontcuberta, Friedrich Kittler, Agnes Varda, Carolee Schneemann, and Hito Steyerl. "Freedom is the strategy of making chance and necessity subordinate to human intention. Freedom is playing against the camera."[13]

Flusser's dystopian view of the future of programs and apparatuses, and the postindustrial universe opening up before us in *Towards a Philosophy of Photography*, is tempered, in the end, by a curious mixture of hope and resignation.

> A philosophy of photography must reveal the fact that there is no place for human freedom within the area of automated, programmed and programming apparatuses, in order finally to show a way in which it is nevertheless possible to open up a space for freedom. The task of a philosophy of photography is to reflect upon this possibility of freedom—and thus its

significance—in a world dominated by apparatuses; to reflect upon the way in which, despite everything, it is possible for human beings to give significance to their lives in face of the chance necessity of death. Such a philosophy is necessary because it is *the only form of revolution left open to us.*[14]

Beyond Belief

After *Towards a Philosophy of Photography*, Flusser went right to work on its sequel, *Ins Universum der technischen Bilder*, published two years later, in 1985. Unfortunately, an English translation was not published until twenty-six years later, in 2011, as *Into the Universe of Technical Images*. Although Flusser meant this volume to be "a continuation and amendment of those arguments articulated in" his earlier essay, *Into the Universe of Technical Images* is very different in tone and intent. Whereas the first book was a cautionary tale, warning against the possible pitfalls of a future cybernetic society (governed by communication and control processes in mechanical and electronic systems, based on feedback), this book exhibits a level of optimism about the telematic world to come that would make Ray Kurzweil blush.[15]

In the opening of this book, Flusser writes that a "future society that synthesizes images … will be a fabulous society, where life is radically different from our own." As in *Towards a Philosophy of Photography*, the stakes are high, and the situation unprecedented: "What is happening around and in us is fantastic, and all previous utopias, whether they were positive or negative, pale in comparison to it."[16] This unprecedented utopia "will no longer be found in any place or time but in imagined surfaces, in surfaces that absorb geography and history." Flusser says that his essay will seek "to grasp this dreaming state of mind as it has begun to crystallize around technical images: the consciousness of a pure information society."[17] It is no wonder that Flusser quickly became a revered and much sought-after prophet of the cybernetic revolution.

When Flusser was writing *Into the Universe of Technical Images*, internet connections were dial-up. The World Wide Web was five years away, smartphones and their cameras were two decades away, and the first widespread social-media platforms even further. But, based on his analysis of photography, Flusser envisioned, with a remarkable particularity and precision, the communications world that we now live in.

Even under the spell of this coming utopia, Flusser continued to insist on the need for criticism, to question the bases of the new order, and to analyze and judge their effects. For him, as always, "the point of cultural criticism is to maintain and increase human freedom and dignity," and he saw how the new order could move toward limiting these principles, especially when it comes to artificial intelligence. "The question of how human intelligence and artificial intelligence are related will become the center of the dialogue very soon. We will face the unpleasant choice between humanizing artificial

intelligence and making human ones move like apparatuses"[18] (remember, this is in 1985). If we make the wrong
choices, the only right we'll have left is the right to say
No, "and this command to stop, this veto right, this right
to say no is the negative decision we call 'freedom.'"[19]

Flusser does not often address the question of belief, per se, but he does write a good deal about doubt.[20]
For my purposes here, doubt is not the opposite of belief, but rather the opposite of certainty. Flusser asserted
that "technical images don't depict anything; they project something," and I think that something projected
is belief. In fact, his ecstatic envisioning of the future
telematic society has a basis in belief; the way he approaches the subject of technical images and media is
infused with questions of belief (in love and death).

Flusser believes that telematics will eventually per-
mit us "to recognize ourselves in others through images
festively, leisurely, without purpose." Robots will do all
the work, and everything humans do will be relaxed, liv-
ing in play, learning, and celebration. Flusser had finally
found an opening to what one of his earliest influences,
Martin Buber, called "dialogic life," writing that the two
possible futures are "a centrally programmed, totalitar-
ian society of image receivers and image administrators,"
or "a dialogic, telematic society of image producers and
image collectors."

Judaism forbade the making of images, and Christianity and Islam, each in its own way, have followed

the same path. This is because images made by human beings obscure the "true image." The "true image" is any human face. It is the image of the absolute other, the "likeness of God." …

All pretelematic images, from Lascaux to video, are discursive, broadcast images, projected against the other, obscuring his face. They are forbidden. They lead the wrong way, away from God. Telematic, dialogically synthesized images, on the other hand, are media between one human being and another, through which I may see the face of the other. And through this face, I may see God.…

We may be at the point of finding our way back, on a strange detour through telematics, to being genuinely human, that is, to a festive existence for another, to purposeless play with others and for others. Even now, we are beginning to be repulsed by pretelematic existence, an existence bound up with purpose and motives, always harping away at what is one's own, as a frightfully serious, joyous, and so profane way of life. A new, completely unorthodox religiosity is beginning to emerge from the musty corners of our consciousness, and this, surprisingly, in the form of the dreamlike universe of technical images.[21]

Flusser sometimes approaches a sort of Gnostic threshold when he contemplates "the implacable tendency of the universe toward disinformation," which would result in "heat death," so "technical images are reservoirs of information that serve our immortality." "The apparatus," he writes, "functions just as the universe does, namely, automatically," which is evil. So we need "envisioners," producers of technical images who "try to turn an automatic apparatus against its own condition of being automatic."

The unrelenting techno-optimism has a pessimistic counter: "The world has become meaningless, and consciousness will find nothing there but so many disconnected elements." Rather than becoming more connected, we are all becoming part of a disconnected world, due to the disappearance of writing and meaning. In the world of technical images, questions about meaning have no answer, because such questions "assume a distinction between true and false, and in the universe of technical images, such distinctions have become superfluous." What's more, any resistance to this new order is futile. "The energy required to withstand the penetrating force of technical images would project such a person out of the social context."

Flusser falls into a best-case, worst-case rhythm. Either the world will be transformed into a free and powerful nirvana, or it will descend into a meaningless morass. He says that "technical images themselves are apocalyptic," but he then makes a call for an intervention to avoid catastrophe: "The traffic between images and people is the central problem of a society ruled by technical images. It is the point where the rising so-called information society may be restructured and made humane."[22]

Flusser always leaves a way out of the morass—into a cultural criticism of the future. "If the point of cultural criticism is to maintain and increase human freedom and dignity, then its focus must be on just these new forms." And "today's revolutionaries are not Khaddaffis or Meinhofs but rather the inventors of technical images. Niépce, Lumière, the numberless and nameless inventors of computer technology, these are the ones who have brought the new social forms about."[23] But "technology has become too serious a matter to be left to technicians."[24]

In contradistinction to *Towards a Philosophy of Photography*, where almost no sources are mentioned in the text, *Into the Universe of Technical Images* is studded with a range of them, including Plato, Hegel, Vico, Schopenhauer, Heidegger, Kierkegaard, Bergson, Buber, Nietzsche, Lacan, Derrida, Deleuze, Guattari, Baudrillard, McLuhan, and Žižek. I've been told that Flusser's traveling library also included works by Giordano Bruno and Jacob Boehme.

*

*   *

I believe that Flusser, especially in *Into the Universe of Technical Images*, vastly underestimated the persistence of the drive for hegemony and control in the form of Surveillance Capitalism and the dangers to democracy in the urge toward technological totality and determinism. But much of his theory about the coming changes to our communications environment has proved sound, and he was really the only one who accurately saw photography, and the photographically derived image (the technical image), at the center of these developments.

The third volume in Flusser's trilogy, *Does Writing Have a Future?* begins this way: "Writing, in the sense of placing letters and other marks one after the other, appears to have little or no future. Information is now more effectively transmitted by codes other than those of written signs."[25] The epochal shift from linear writing and literacy to technical images is transforming the world, just as the rise of linear writing and widespread literacy transformed Greece in the fourth and fifth centuries BC.[26] It is my contention that this epochal shift is significantly affecting and being affected by the relation between photography and belief. How do we believe technical images, and how is that belief changing?

Chapter 4

Three Sources

To understand how and why we believe photographic images, technical images, the way we do, and how this credulity allows us to be manipulated by these images, we must look to the distant past, long before the invention of technical images, because it is clear that when technical images were invented, old image-beliefs were transferred onto them. These old image-beliefs come from the time before the era of "art," when images were seen to be not *representations* but *emanations*. This pre-art legacy of the *acheiropoetic* image (the image not made by hand) was picked up by technical images. Even as they lost their Benjaminian "aura," they gained another, the aura of *belief*. Even though photographs inherited the *acheiropoetic* status—and people generally wanted to think of photographs as being more "real" and more believable than images made by hand—photographs are and always have been more fiction than fact.

And so I triangulated among three sources that offer insight into such a legacy: Vilém Flusser's *Towards a Philosophy of Photography*, Ioan P. Couliano's *Eros and Magic in the Renaissance*, and Hans Belting's *Likeness and Presence: A History of the Image Before the Era of Art.*

As we have seen, Flusser's book is a phenomenological approach to technical images—an attempt to understand what these things are and how they operate. Whereas Flusser defines magic as "a form of existence corresponding to the eternal recurrence of the same," in contrast to history, and imagination as "the specific ability to produce and to decode images," Couliano defines magic as "a science of the imaginary":

> At its greatest degree of development, reached in the work of Giordano Bruno, magic is a means of control over the individual and the masses based on deep knowledge of personal and collective erotic impulses.... The magician of the Renaissance is both psychoanalyst and prophet as well as the precursor of modern professions such as director of public relations, propagandist, spy, politician, censor, director of mass communication media, and publicity agent.[1]

Couliano believed that the shift from a society dominated by magic to one dominated by science is primarily "a change in the imaginary," and that the European scientific revolution that led to the annihilation of the Renaissance sciences was "caused by *religious* factors which have nothing to do with the sciences themselves."[2] "Because magic relied upon the use of images, and images were repressed and banned in the Reformation and subsequent history, magic was replaced by exact science and modern technology and eventually forgotten."

Belting, in his thoroughly useful history of the image, writes that when old images were destroyed by the iconoclasts in the Reformation, in the sixteenth century, "images of a new kind began to fill the art collections which were just then being formed."[3] Thus began the era of art, which continues to this day. Before this era, sacred icons and other cult images were not thought to be the work of artists, but were believed to be either "of heavenly origin or produced by mechanical impression during the lifetime of the model."[4] It is the latter type of *acheiropoetic* image that I believe is the progenitor of technical images.

Both Flusser and Couliano are writing into what they see as a social crisis, and both raise cries of alarm. Couliano's book "examines changes at the level of the *imaginary* rather than at the level of scientific *discoveries*," and finds that

> nowadays, if we can boast of having at our disposal scientific knowledge and technology that used to exist only in the phantasies of magicians, we must allow that, since the Renaissance, our capacity to work directly with our own phantasms, if not with those of others, has diminished. The relationship between the conscious and the unconscious has been deeply altered and *our ability to control our own processes of imagination* reduced to nothing."[5]

For Couliano, the historical record is clear: "The revolution in spirit and customs brought about by the Reformation led to the total destruction of Renaissance ideals. The Renaissance conceived of the natural and social world as a spiritual organism in which perpetual exchanges of phantasmic messages occurred. That was the principle of magic and of Eros, Eros itself being a form of magic." He sees this not as a "mere curiosity of history, but illuminating proof that our civilization continues to die in the trenches dug by the Reformation and by the political events that followed it. The modern West—as Nietzsche foresaw—is assuming the character of a *fatal* result of the Reformation. But is it also the *final* result, its lines of development fixed, once and for all, in the sixteenth and seventeenth centuries?"[6] On this question Couliano's book closes, as he writes, "without daring to express too clearly a hope that may be utopian: that a new Renaissance, a rebirth of the world, may overcome all our neuroses, all conflicts, and all divisions existing between us. For such a Renaissance to appear a new Reformation must arise, effecting once again a profound modification of the human imagination in order to impress on it other paths and other goals."[7]

Ultimately, I'm interested in the ways we respond to and are manipulated by technical images, and I am more and more convinced that the key to this is magical, in Flusser's sense of "a form of existence corresponding to the eternal recurrence of the same," Couliano's sense of magic as "a science of the imaginary," and in Bruno's sense as "a means of control over the individual and the masses based on deep knowledge of personal and collective erotic impulses." Flusser's sense of magic is post-historical here, coming into play after the historical narrative of progress is broken and images come to displace texts. In this context, our belief about images—that they are emanations of the referent, for example—pushes our relations with images into the realm of magic, if we can extract magic from Eurocentric and colonialist ideas about "primitive thought" and modify the functionalist approach to magic by Marcel Mauss and Émile Durkheim to account for recent changes in the ontology of images.

The connection between magic and technology has long been a preoccupation of continental philosophy, and it may finally be coming back into focus.[8] One foundational strand of this is the ethnographic grounding of magic as social fact by Marcel Mauss,[9] and its updating and skeptical enhancing by Michael Taussig, whereby "rites of exposure [are] built into rites of magic in order to strengthen magic itself."[10] But it was Vilém Flusser who brought magic back into the philosophy of photography.

Chapter 5

Without a Future:
Post-Photography and the Problem of Belief

I love photographs. That means I believe them. It does not mean I am gullible about images, or that I am more susceptible to fakery or propaganda. And it does not mean that I am uncritical or unthinking in my relation to photographs.

I am a realist in the same way Barthes is; that is, I "do not take the photograph for a 'copy' of reality, but for an emanation of *past reality*: a *magic*, not an art." And I believe, with Flusser, that there has been a great deal of ontological confusion about photography from its inception, and that it was, in fact, the first manifestation of the cybernetic future of media. The camera was the first telematic device. When the camera became ubiquitous, on cell phones and tablets, it led to a new stage in the development of technical images. Obviously, more technical images are produced every day than ever before.

It is also commonly understood that human beings today consume more technical images than at any previous time. This is certainly, objectively, numerically true, but I would argue that this consumption is different in kind from that of an earlier time. Images that appear on the screens of our devices go by in a streaming *flow*. Individual images are seldom apprehended separately, as a singular *trace*. Singular, still images operate very differently on the mind. The images consumed in a flow are seldom dwelled on, so their individual effect is limited, creating instead a disproportionately generalized effect. This generalized effect has been under-theorized,[1] just as the effect of words and images working together has been. It can further be argued that this flow of images has a less concentrated, singular effect than previous practices that involved discrete images being viewed repeatedly over time.

The "photographs" we take with our smartphones are highly processed images, as are the photograph-like images of black holes and galaxies constructed from information collected using a vast network of radio telescopes. In fact, the vast majority of technical images produced today are not intended for human reception at all, but are device-to-device communications. Big information transfers are increasingly carried out through images, not text.

A contemporaneous counterpoint to technical images functioning independently from human perception, device to device, is the case of personal photos that are never printed. These personal images, however numerous, remain data points, accumulating independently under a lack of reception and, consequently, a lack of belief. Belief requires making a connection, some reciprocity. Photography is a reciprocal intervention, and so involves belief. Data-driven information can be autonomous accumulation, the Spectacle that Debord recognized as "Capital becoming image." Capital has turned being into having, and having into appearing, and it has turned appearances into a commodity, leading to estrangement and alienation. If we are going to reestablish a connection to the world, a belief in the world, we have to be able to see it "in a glass, darkly," on the way to a face-to-face.

Every time a new technology involving the manipulation of technical images appears, there is a "sky is falling" response, claiming that we are entering a post-truth environment and can no longer believe our eyes. We're seeing it now in response to AI-generated "deepfake" videos, which first appeared on Reddit as pornographic videos with celebrities' heads transplanted onto anonymous bodies, and then moved on to depicting politicians saying untoward things. In June 2019, the U.S. House of Representatives Intelligence Committee held a hearing on the threat that "deepfake" videos pose to national security.

Granted, the stakes in this struggle against deepfake manipulations are unquestionably high. If you gain concentrated control over large communications apparatuses, you can convince masses of people to do almost anything, and distorting the significance of events and destroying credibility is an essential part of that. Hannah Arendt laid it out in 1951, in *The Origins of Totalitarianism*: if you want to destroy people's ability to resist control, you must destroy the distinction between truth and lies, because if you can't *believe* anything, you can't *act*.

In technological, political, and social terms, it seems that reality is increasingly under siege. Paul Virilio was characteristically prescient when he wrote, in 1997, that "it is becoming hard, even impossible, to believe in the stability of the real, in our ability to pin down a visible that never stops vanishing."[2] At times, it seems that technical images are lifting off and separating from the surfaces of our screens, becoming even further disconnected from the real.

But, again, the truth is that photographs have always been manipulated and faked. Only the methods change. And a certain kind of overreaction to these changes indicates a fundamental misunderstanding of the relation between images and belief, and the way we believe technical images, in particular. This belief is transitive. It is a *willed* belief. Photographs are complex and fascinating because of the ways we believe them. Belief does not arise from the object of the photograph. It comes from the subject, from us.

This is not to say that technological developments do not affect the epistemic utility of technical images, as the way people receive them changes. As the aura of believability fades from technical images, their bond with the referent loosens. Visual images become more like testimony than like perception. This makes it imperative to know the origins of a given image: Who made it, for what purpose? It also makes it more difficult to assess responses to technical images based on their truth claims. Our unbridled belief in the primacy of technology has caused a concomitant decline in our belief in human desires and capabilities.

Historically, beliefs do not disappear. Instead, they are projected onto different objects. We no longer be-

lieve in gods and heroes, but we believe in celebrities. We
no longer believe in magic, but we believe in technology.
We no longer believe in reality, but we believe in images.

*

*   *

What characterizes the so-called advanced societies
is that they today consume images and no longer, like
those of the past, beliefs. —Barthes, *Camera Lucida*

[Images] are supposed to be maps but they turn into
screens. Instead of representing the world, they obscure it, until human beings' lives finally become a
function of the images they create. —Flusser, *Towards
a Philosophy of Photography*

*

*   *

Belief in images has become the test case for the social.
If we do not find a way to believe what we see in images,
we will lose the ability to act socially. Belief involves "an
ethic of otherness."[3] And belief requires will. Like love.
Falling in love is not exactly a choice, but at some point,
will comes into it.

If we are to believe in the world, we must have images of it, and we must have something to do with those
images. I don't know how that will be accomplished

technically in the future, or whether that new way will be "photographic," but it will certainly draw on the age-old belief in images, from the caves forward.

Benjamin, Berger, and Barthes all write of the melancholic nature of photography and of its inherent connection to death. At one point in *Camera Lucida*, Barthes writes that the photograph "is *without future* (this is its pathos, its melancholy)."[4] With Flusser, it's even more eschatologically dire.

As technical images increasingly shift from the trace to the flow, the photograph may ultimately become obsolete. But the desire for such images will not disappear. This desire may be projected onto other kinds of technical images, or onto some future trace mechanism designed to fix and conserve internal images, or images in the mind. Whatever forms these new images take, the question of belief—how and why we believe them—will remain critical.

A Brief Anthology of Quotations on
Photography and Belief
[Homage to Walter Benjamin and Susan Sontag]

"The true mystery of the world is the visible."—Oscar Wilde

"We must take literally what vision teaches us: namely, that through it we come in contact with the sun and the stars, that we are everywhere all at once, and that even our power to imagine ourselves elsewhere … borrows from vision and employs means we owe to it." —Maurice Merleau-Ponty, *The Primacy of Perception* (1964)

"Hearers tell of what they hear, observers [seers] really know." —Plautus, *Truculentus*, 2.6 (c. 299 BC)

"What is a miracle? It's something that is being given so that one believes, so that there would be a superior hope." —Paul Virilio, *Crepuscular Dawn* (2002)

"Some years ago I was struck by how many false things I had believed, and by how doubtful was the structure of beliefs that I had based on them…. Yet although the senses sometimes deceive us about objects that are very small or distant, that doesn't apply to my belief that I am here, sitting by the fire, wearing a winter dressing-gown, holding this piece of paper in my hands, and so on. It seems to be quite impossible to doubt beliefs like these, which come from the senses." —René Descartes, *Meditations on First Philosophy* (1641)

"Many are those who trade in tricks and simulated miracles, duping the foolish multitude; and if nobody unmasked their subterfuges, they would impose them on everyone." —Leonardo da Vinci, manuscript F in the Library of the Institut de France

"The amazing growth of our techniques, the adaptability and precision they have attained, the idea and habits they are creating, make it a certainty that profound changes are impending in the ancient craft of the Beautiful." —Paul Valéry, quoted by Benjamin in an epigraph to the "Work of Art" essay

"Now faith is the substance of things hoped for, the evidence of things not seen." —Saint Paul, Hebrews 11:1

Fox Talbot called photography "evidence of a novel kind."

In the Marx Brothers' film *Duck Soup* (1933), Mrs. Teasdale (Margaret Dumont) insists on what she has seen with her own eyes, and Chicolini (Chico Marx), who, along with his brothers, has been engaged in an elaborate visual hoax, says, "Well, who you gonna believe? Me or your own eyes?"

"I wouldn't have seen it
if I hadn't believed it."
—Variously ascribed on the internet to Marshall McLuhan, Yogi Berra, and George Bernard Shaw

"The seemingly irreconcilable difference between theories of knowledge and theories of belief demonstrates that the psychology of the image-spectator is an inextricable mixture of knowledge and belief." —Jacques Aumont, *The Image* (1997)

"And don't forget that the structure of the atom cannot be seen but is nonetheless known. I know about lots of things I've never seen. And so do you. You can't show proof of the truest thing of all, all you can do is believe. Weep and believe." —Clarice Lispector, *The Hour of the Star*, translated by Benjamin Moser (1977)

The main character in J. M. Coetzee's novel *Elizabeth Costello* "no longer believes very strongly in belief.... Belief may be no more … than a … battery which one clips into an idea to make it run."

"The advocacy of what we believe in is education. The advocacy of what we don't believe in is propaganda." —Edward Bernays, the inventor of modern public relations

"I say then that likenesses of things and their shapes are given off by things from the outermost body of things, which may be called, as it were, films or even rind, because the image bears an appearance and form like to that, whatever it be, from whose body it appears to be shed, ere it wanders abroad. That we may learn from this, however dull be our wits." —*Lucretius on the Nature of Things*, book 4, lines 48–54, translated by Cyril Bailey (Oxford, 1924)

"If anyone had come and told Napoleon that a man or a building is incessantly, and at all hours, represented by an image in the atmosphere, that all existing objects have there a kind of specter which can be captured and perceived, he would have consigned him to Charenton as a lunatic.... Yet that is what Daguerre's discovery proved." —Honoré de Balzac, *Le Cousin Pons*, in *Oeuvres complètes*, vol. 18, *La Comédie humaine: Scènes de la vie parisienne*, 6 (Paris, 1914), pp. 129–130 [quoted in "Convolute Y," in *The Arcades Project*, p. 688]

"No one can say what will be 'real' for people when the wars which are now beginning come to an end." —Werner Heisenberg (epigraph to Paul Virilio's *The Information Bomb*)

"[The masses] do not believe in anything visible, in the reality of their own experience; they do not trust their eyes and ears but only their imaginations, which may be caught by anything that is at once universal and consistent in itself. What convinces masses are not facts, and not even invented facts, but only the consistency of the system of which they are presumably part. Repetition, somewhat overrated in importance because of the common belief in the masses' inferior capacity to grasp and remember, is important only because it convinces them of consistency in time." —Hannah Arendt, *The Origins of Totalitarianism* (2004)

"Looking out for one's own interests is no substitute for belief.... Believing is being exhausted. Or at least it takes refuge in the areas of the media and leisure activities." —Michel de Certeau, *The Practice of Everyday Life* (1984)

"But the thing a man does practically believe (and this is often enough *without* asserting it even to himself, much less to others); the thing a man does practically lay to heart, and know for certain, concerning his vital relations to this mysterious Universe, and his duty and destiny there, that is in all cases the primary thing for him, and creatively determines all the rest. That is his *religion*; or it may be, his mere skepticism and *no-religion*: the manner it is in which he feels himself to be spiritually related to the Unseen World or No-World; and I say, if you tell me what that is, you tell me to a very great extent what the man is, what the kind of things he will do is." —Thomas Carlyle, *On Heroes, Hero-Worship, and the Heroic in History* (1841)

"The real problem of modernity is the problem of belief." —Daniel Bell, *The Cultural Contradictions of Capitalism* (1976)

"But certainly for the present age, which prefers the sign to the thing signified, the copy to the original, representation to reality, the appearance to the essence ... *illusion* only is sacred, *truth* profane. Nay, sacredness is held to be enhanced in proportion as truth decreases and illusion increases, so that the highest degree of illusion comes to be the highest degree of sacredness." —Ludwig Feuerbach, preface to the second edition of *The Essence of Christianity* (1843), used by Guy Debord as the epigraph to *The Society of the Spectacle* (1967)

"Truth is image, but there is no image of truth." —Marie-José Mondzain

"Photography and philosophy are both methods of methodically dealing with *doubt* (the search for a standpoint to generate an image = idea)." —Vilém Flusser, letter to Milton Vargas, July 20, 1975

"We regard the photograph, the picture on our wall, as the object itself (the man, the landscape, and so on) depicted there.
　"This need not have been so. We could easily imagine people who did not have this relation to such pictures. Who, for example, would be repelled by photographs, because a face without color and even perhaps a face in reduced proportions struck them as inhuman." —Ludwig Wittgenstein, *Philosophical Investigations*

"With the daguerreotype everyone will be able to have their portrait taken—formerly it was only the prominent; and at the same time everything is being done to make us all look exactly the same—so that we shall only need one portrait." —Søren Kierkegaard, 1854

"In the spring of 1921, two automatic photographic machines, recently invented abroad, were installed in Prague, which reproduced six or ten or more exposures of the same person on a single print.

"When I took such a series of photographs to Kafka I said light-heartedly: 'For a couple of krone one can have oneself photographed from every angle. The apparatus is a mechanical Know-Thyself.'

"'You mean to say, the *Mistake-Thyself*,' said Kafka, with a faint smile." —Gustav Janouch, *Conversations with Kafka*, translated by Goronwy Rees (1971)

"'Not being able to believe your eyes' is no longer, in fact, a sign of amazement or surprise, but rather a mark of a 'conscientious objection' that now objects to the hold of the objective image, of the image mediatized not only by the live or recently pre-recorded TV broadcast, but also by an excessive *mobilization of public space* in which moving stairways and walkways are the missing link in the chain that leads from public transport's automobilization of the domestic household to the lift in the high-rise tower of the wired smart building....

"*Since the optical unwinding of the reel now no longer lets up*, it is becoming hard, even impossible, to believe in the stability of the real, in our ability to pin down a visible that never stops vanishing, the space of the building suddenly giving way to the instability of a public image that has become omnipresent." —Paul Virilio, *Open Sky* (1997)

"Love bears all things, believes all things, hopes all things, endures all things.... For now we see through a glass, darkly; but then face to face." —1 Corinthians 13:7 (Revised Standard Version) and 12 (King James Bible)

Notes

Chapter 1

1   Kristeva, "Ellipsis on Terror and the Specular Seduction," pp. 42–47.
2   Strauss, "Photography and Belief" in *Between the Eyes*, p. 73.
3   Benveniste, *Dictionary of Indo-European Concepts and Society*, p. 134.
4   Agamben, Foreword, in Benveniste, *Dictionary of Indo-European Concepts and Society*, p. xiv.
5   All verses from the Bible cited in this volume are from the Revised Standard Version, unless otherwise indicated.
6   Sontag, *Regarding the Pain of Others*.
7   Berger, "Where Are We?" in *Between the Eyes*, by David Levi Strauss, p. x. See also two reviews of *Between the Eyes*: Peter Wollen, "Shooting Wars," *The Nation*, October 6, 2003, p. 57; and Jeremy Harding, "Humanitarian Art," *The London Review of Books*, August 21, 2003, pp. 22–23.
8   Duchamp, *Duchamp du signe*, p. 185.
9   Most, *Doubting Thomas*, p. 34.
10   Most, *Doubting Thomas*, p. 28.
11   Most, *Doubting Thomas*, p. 214.
12   Luther, *Luther's Large Catechism*, Article 114.
13   See Ricoeur, "The Image of God and the Epic of Man."
14   Kristeva, "Ellipsis on Terror and the Specular Seduction," p. 46.
15   Picknett and Prince apparently wrote their book, *Turin Shroud: In Whose Image? The Shocking Truth Behind the Centuries-Long Conspiracy of Silence*, with no knowledge of Nicholas Allen's research.
16   Pope John Paul II, as quoted in Latour and Weibel, *Iconoclash: Beyond the Image Wars in Science, Religion, and Art*, pp. 236–238 (emphasis added).
17   Allen, "The Methods and Techniques Employed in the Manufacture of the Shroud of Turin."
18   In 1987, the computer-art pioneer Lillian F. Schwartz demonstrated that the face of the Mona Lisa lines up perfectly with the face of Leonardo in his self-portrait. Later, Schwartz went some way to show that the face on the shroud (and the one in the recently heralded *Salvatore Mundi*) also matches up with Leonardo's visage. Obviously, this is all before recent advances in facial-recognition technology.
19   Picknett and Prince, *Turin Shroud*, pp. 147–148.
20   See Fetzer, *The Great Zapruder Film Hoax: Deceit and Deception in the Death of JFK*.

Chapter 2

1 Leslie, Introduction to "Small History of Photography," in Benjamin, *On Photography*, p. 55. See also Benjamin, *The Correspondence of Walter Benjamin, 1910–1940*, p. 385.

2 Benjamin, "Small History of Photography," in *On Photography*, pp. 61–62.

3 Benjamin, "Small History of Photography," in *On Photography*, p. 68 (emphasis added).

4 Benjamin, "Small History of Photography," in *On Photography*, p. 83. In "The Work of Art in the Age of Mechanical Reproduction," in Benjamin, *Illuminations: Essays and Reflections*, Benjamin defines the aura similarly as "the unique phenomenon of a distance, however close it may be" (p. 222). The aura is uniqueness, in unapproachability (aesthetic distance).

5 Benjamin, "Small History of Photography," in *On Photography*, p. 84.

6 Benjamin, "Small History of Photography," in *On Photography*, pp. 84–85.

7 Susan Sontag's *On Photography* came out in 1977, from Farrar, Straus and Giroux, and Roland Barthes's *Camera Lucida: Reflections on Photography* appeared in Richard Howard's translation in 1981, also from Farrar, Straus and Giroux.

8 Berger, "Appearances," in Berger and Mohr, *Another Way of Telling*, p. 99.

9 Berger's ire here is matched by Benjamin's in response to the photography of Albert Renger-Patzsch in *Die Welt ist schön* (The World Is Beautiful): "It reveals the attitude of a photography that can fit any tin can into the universe but can grasp none of the human relationships in which it appears, and which thereby, even in its most dreamlike subjects, is merely a harbinger of its saleability rather than its recognition" (Benjamin, *On Photography*, p. 91). Benjamin also calls photography "the first truly revolutionary means of reproduction," arising "simultaneously with the rise of socialism" (Benjamin, *Illuminations*, p. 224).

10 Berger, "Appearances," in Berger and Mohr, *Another Way of Telling*, p. 100.

11 Berger, "Appearances," in Berger and Mohr, *Another Way of Telling*, p. 100.

12 Berger, "Appearances," in Berger and Mohr, *Another Way of Telling*, p. 96.

13 Berger, "Appearances," in Berger and Mohr, *Another Way of Telling*, p. 97.

14 This puts him, briefly, in dialogue with Barthes's *Camera Lucida* (p. 112).

15 Berger, "Appearances," in Berger and Mohr, *Another Way of Telling*, p. 129.

16 Berger, "Appearances," in Berger and Mohr, *Another Way of Telling*, p. 108.

17 Barthes, *Camera Lucida*, p. 3.

18 Barthes, *Camera Lucida*, p. 82.

19 Barthes, *Camera Lucida*, pp. 87–88.

20 Barthes, *Camera Lucida*, p. 88.

21 Barthes, *Camera Lucida*, p. 119.

22 Silverman, *The Miracle of Analogy, or The History of Photography*, p. 164.

23 Daguerre, as quoted in Silverman, *The Miracle of Analogy, or The History of Photography*, p. 26.
24 Fox Talbot, as quoted in Silverman, *The Miracle of Analogy, or The History of Photography*, p. 26.
25 Silverman, *The Miracle of Analogy, or The History of Photography*, pp. 10–11.
26 Barthes, *Camera Lucida*, pp. 88–89.
27 Janouch, *Conversations with Kafka*, p. 152.
28 Gunning, "What's the Point of an Index?," pp. 39–49.
29 Gunning, "What's the Point of an Index?," p. 46.
30 Gunning, "What's the Point of an Index?," p. 48.

Chapter 3

1 Flusser, *Towards a Philosophy of Photography*, p. 7.
2 Flusser, *Towards a Philosophy of Photography*, p. 9.
3 Flusser, *Towards a Philosophy of Photography*, p. 13.
4 Flusser, *Towards a Philosophy of Photography*, p. 20.
5 Flusser, *Towards a Philosophy of Photography*, p. 25.
6 Flusser, *Towards a Philosophy of Photography*, p. 30.
7 Flusser, *Towards a Philosophy of Photography*, p. 58.
8 Flusser, *Towards a Philosophy of Photography*, p. 64.
9 Flusser, *Towards a Philosophy of Photography*, p. 49.
10 Flusser, *Towards a Philosophy of Photography*, p. 70.
11 Flusser, *Towards a Philosophy of Photography*, p. 71.
12 Flusser, *Towards a Philosophy of Photography*, p. 74.
13 Flusser, *Towards a Philosophy of Photography*, p. 80.
14 Flusser, *Towards a Philosophy of Photography*, pp. 81–82 (emphasis added).
15 The mathematician and philosopher Norbert Weiner was the originator of cybernetics (from the Greek, to "steer" or "govern"). His work had a tremendous influence on that of the anthropologists Gregory Bateson and Margaret Mead, and on the poet Charles Olson. The American inventor and futurist Ray Kurzweil has written extensively on artificial intelligence, transhumanism, the technological singularity, and life extension. He is a director of engineering at Google.
16 Flusser, *Into the Universe*, p. 3.
17 Flusser, *Into the Universe*, p. 4.
18 Flusser, *Into the Universe*, p. 113.
19 Flusser, *Into the Universe*, p. 122.
20 One of Flusser's major early Brazilian works is *Da dúvida* (On Doubt), written in the mid-1960s, but not published until 1999, and in a full English translation, by Rodrigo Maltez Novaes, and edited by Siegfried Zielinski, in 2014, as *On Doubt*. "In the preface to the 1999 edition, Celso Lafer mentions that in 1965 when he was a student at Cornell University, he gave a

German version of *A düvida* to Hannah Arendt at Flusser's request. Lafer mentions that he had the opportunity to look at the text with Arendt and discuss the contents" (p. x).

21 Flusser, *Into the Universe*, pp. 156–157.
22 Flusser, *Into the Universe*, p. 60.
23 Flusser, *Into the Universe*, p. 63.
24 Flusser, *Into the Universe*, p. 65.
25 Flusser, *Does Writing Have a Future?*, p. 3.
26 See Havelock, *Preface to Plato*.

Chapter 4

1 Couliano, *Eros and Magic in the Renaissance*, p. xviii.
2 Couliano, *Eros and Magic in the Renaissance*, p. xx.
3 Belting, *Likeness and Presence*, p. xxi.
4 Belting, *Likeness and Presence*, p. 49.
5 Couliano, *Eros and Magic in the Renaissance*, p. xix (emphasis added).
6 Couliano, *Eros and Magic in the Renaissance*, p. 223.
7 Couliano, *Eros and Magic in the Renaissance*, p. 223.
8 See, for instance, Campagna, *Technic and Magic*.
9 See Mauss, *A General Theory of Magic*.
10 Taussig, "Viscerality, Faith, and Skepticism," in *Walter Benjamin's Grave*, p. 148.

Chapter 5

1 Guy Debord's *The Society of the Spectacle* (1967) remains a necessary base: "The spectacle is not a collection of images; rather, it is a social relationship between people that is mediated by images"; and "The spectacle is capital accumulated to the point where it becomes an image." In his preface to the third French edition of *The Society of the Spectacle* in 1992, Debord said he would not change anything in the book, because "a critical theory of the kind presented here needed no changing—not as long, at any rate, as the general conditions of the long historical period that it was the first to describe accurately were still intact. The continued unfolding of our epoch has merely confirmed and further illustrated the theory of the spectacle." I think that assessment is still valid in 2020.
2 Virilio, *Open Sky*, p. 90.
3 Blaser, "Bach's Belief," in *The Fire: Collected Essays of Robin Blaser*, p. 352.
4 Barthes, *Camera Lucida*, p. 90.

Bibliography

Agamben, Giorgio. *Stanzas: Word & Phantasm in Western Culture*. Minneapolis: University of Minnesota Press, 1993. See esp. chap. 5, "The Phantasms of Eros," and chap. 13, "Spiritus phantasticus."

Allen, Nicholas. "The Methods and Techniques Employed in the Manufacture of the Shroud of Turin." PhD diss., University of Durban-Westville, 1993. https://researchspace.ukzn.ac.za/xmlui/bitstream/handle/10413/8589/Allen_Nicholas_P_L_1993.pdf?sequence=1&isAllowed=y.

Arendt, Hannah. *The Origins of Totalitarianism*. New York: Schocken Books, 2004.

Aumont, Jacques. *The Image*. Translated by Claire Pajackowska. London: British Film Institute, 1997. See esp. "Knowledge and Belief."

Barthes, Roland. *Camera Lucida: Reflections on Photography*. Translated by Richard Howard. New York: Hill and Wang/Farrar, Straus and Giroux, 1981.

Bazin, André. "The Ontology of the Photographic Image." In *What Is Cinema?*, pp. 9–16. Translated by Hugh Gray. Berkeley, CA: University of California Press, 1971.

Belting, Hans. *Likeness and Presence: A History of the Image Before the Era of Art*. Translated by Edmund Jephcott. Chicago: University of Chicago Press, 1994.

Benjamin, Walter. "Convolute Y [Photography]." In *The Arcades Project*, pp. 671–692. Translated by Howard Eiland and Kevin McLaughlin. Cambridge, MA: Belknap Press of Harvard University Press, 1999.

———. *The Correspondence of Walter Benjamin, 1910–1940*. Edited and annotated by Gershom Scholem and Theodor W. Adorno. Translated by Manfred R. Jacobson and Evelyn M. Jacobson. Chicago: University of Chicago Press, 1994.

———. *Illuminations: Essays and Reflections*. Edited by Hannah Arendt. Translated by Harry Zohn. New York: Schocken Books, 1969.

———. *On Photography*. Edited and translated by Esther Leslie. London: Reaktion Books, 2015.

———. *One-Way Street and Other Writings*. Translated by Edmund Jephcott and Kingsley Shorter. London: New Left Books, 1979.

Benveniste, Émile. *Dictionary of Indo-European Concepts and Society*. Translated by Elizabeth Palmer. Foreword by Giorgio Agamben. Reprint. Chicago: HAU Books, 2016.

Berger, John. *Understanding a Photograph*. Edited and with an introduction by Geoff Dyer. New York: Aperture, 2013.

———. Introduction to *Between the Eyes: Essays on Photography and Politics*, by David Levi Strauss, pp. vii–xv. New York: Aperture, 2003.

Berger, John, and Jean Mohr. *Another Way of Telling*. New York: Pantheon, 1982.

Blaser, Robin. "Bach's Belief" and "The Irreparable." In *The Fire: Collected*

Essays of Robin Blaser, pp. 350–367; pp. 98–110. Edited by Miriam Nichols. Berkeley, CA: University of California Press, 2006.

Bruno, Giordano. *On the Composition of Images, Signs & Ideas*. Edited and annotated by Dick Higgins. Translated by Charles Doria. New York: Willis, Locker & Owens, 1991.

Campagna, Federico. *Technic and Magic*. London: Bloomsbury Academic, 2018.

Campbell, Stephen J. "Twilight of the Idol: Martin Luther, Art History, and the Disenchantment of Art." *Bookforum*, October/November 2004.

Certeau, Michel de. *The Practice of Everyday Life*. Translated by Steven Rendall. Berkeley, CA: University of California Press, 1984. See esp. part 5, chap. 13, "Believing and Making People Believe."

Couliano, Ioan P. *Eros and Magic in the Renaissance*. Translated by Margaret Cook. Chicago: University of Chicago Press, 1987.

Danto, Arthur C. "When Seeing Was Believing." *The Nation*, March 7, 2005.

Debord, Guy. *Comments on the Society of the Spectacle*. Translated by Malcolm Imrie. London: Verso, 1998.

———. *Panegyric*. Translated by James Brook and John McHale. 2 vols. London: Verso, 2004.

———. *The Society of the Spectacle and Other Films*. 1967. Translated by Donald Nicholson-Smith. New York: Zone Books, 1994.

Duchamp, Marcel. *Duchamp du signe*. Paris: Flammarion, 1975.

Ellul, Jacques. *Propaganda: The Formation of Men's Attitudes*. Translated by Konrad Kellen and Jean Lerner. New York: Vintage Books, 1973.

Fetzer, James H., ed. *The Great Zapruder Film Hoax: Deceit and Deception in the Death of JFK*. Chicago: Catfeet Press, 2003.

Feurerbach, Ludwig. *The Essence of Christianity*. Translated by George Eliot. Reprint. Mineola, NY: Dover Publications, 2008.

Flusser, Vilém. *Does Writing Have a Future?* Translated by Nancy Ann Roth. Minneapolis, MN: University of Minnesota Press, 2011.

———. *The Holy See: An Extract from The Last Judgment, Generations*. Translated and with an introduction by Rodrigo Maltez Novaes. Pittsburgh: Flugschriften, 2019.

———. *Into the Universe of Technical Images*. Translated by Nancy Ann Roth. Minneapolis, MN: University of Minnesota Press, 2011.

———. *On Doubt*. Edited by Sigfried Zielinski. Translated by Rodrigo Maltez Novaes. Minneapolis, MN: Univocal, 2014.

———. *The Surprising Phenomenon of Human Communication*. Edited by Rodrigo Maltez Novaes. Lavergne, TN: Metaflux Publishing, 2016.

———. *Towards a Philosophy of Photography*. Translated by Anthony Mathews. London: Reaktion Books, 2000.

Freedberg, David. *The Power of Images: Studies in the History and Theory of Response*. Chicago: University of Chicago Press, 1989.

Groys, Boris. *In the Flow*. London: Verso, 2016.

Gunning, Tom. "Phantom Images and Modern Manifestations: Spirit Photography, Magic Theater, Trick Films, and Photography's Uncanny." In *Fugitive Images: From Photography to Video*, pp. 42–71. Edited by Patrice Petro. Bloomington, IN: Indiana University Press, 1995.

———. "What's the Point of an Index? or, Faking Photography." *Nordicom Review* 25, nos. 1–2 (January 2004): 39–49.

Harding, Jeremy. "Humanitarian Art." *The London Review of Books* 25, no. 16 (August 21, 2003): 22–23.

Havelock, Eric A. *Preface to Plato*. Cambridge, MA: Belknap Press of Harvard University Press, 1963.

Heidegger, Martin. *The Question Concerning Technology and Other Essays*. Translated and with an introduction by William Lovitt. New York: Harper and Row, 1977.

Janouch, Gustav. *Conversations with Kafka*. Translated by Goronwy Rees. New York: New Directions, 1971.

Koerner, Joseph Leo. *The Reformation of the Image.* Chicago: University of Chicago Press, 2004. See esp. "Beliefs."

Kristeva, Julia. "Ellipsis on Terror and the Specular Seduction." Translated by Dolores Burdick. *Wide Angle* 3:2 (1979). Originally published as "Ellipse sur la frayeur et la séduction spéculaire." *Communications* 23 (1975): 73–78.

Latour, Bruno, and Peter Weibel, eds. *Iconoclash: Beyond the Image Wars in Science, Religion, and Art*. Karlsruhe, Germany, and Cambridge, MA: ZKM and The MIT Press, 2002. See esp. "Address of His Holiness Pope John Paul II, Sunday, 24 May 1998."

Luther, Martin. *Luther's Large Catechism*. Minneapolis, MN: Augsburg, 1935.

Mauss, Marcel. *A General Theory of Magic*. Translated by Robert Brain. London: Routledge and Kegan Paul, 1972.

Mondzain, Marie-José. *Image, Icon, Economy: The Byzantine Origins of the Contemporary Imaginary*. Translated by Rico Franses. Stanford, CA: Stanford University Press, 2005.

Most, Glenn W. *Doubting Thomas*. Cambridge, MA: Harvard University Press, 2005.

Nancy, Jean-Luc. *The Ground of the Image*. Translated by Jeff Fort. New York: Fordham University Press, 2005.

Nochlin, Linda. *Realism*. Harmondsworth, England: Penguin Books, 1971.

Picknett, Lynn, and Clive Prince. *Turin Shroud: In Whose Image? The Shocking Truth Behind the Centuries-Long Conspiracy of Silence*. New York: HarperCollins, 1994.

Ricoeur, Paul. "The Image of God and the Epic of Man." *CrossCurrents* 11, no. 1 (Winter 1961): 37–50.

Silverman, Kaja. *The Miracle of Analogy, or the History of Photography, Part 1*. Stanford, CA: Stanford University Press, 2015.

Sontag, Susan. *On Photography*. New York: Farrar, Straus and Giroux, 1977.

———. *Regarding the Pain of Others*. New York: Farrar, Straus and Giroux, 2003.

Steyerl, Hito. *Duty Free Art: Art in the Age of Planetary Civil War*. London: Verso, 2017.

Strauss, David Levi. "Photography and Belief." In *Between the Eyes: Essays on Photography and Politics*, pp. 71–78. Introduction by John Berger. New York: Aperture, 2003.

Taussig, Michael. "Viscerality, Faith, and Skepticism: Another Theory of Magic." In *Walter Benjamin's Grave*, pp. 121–155. Chicago: University of Chicago Press, 2006.

Virilio, Paul. *The Information Bomb*. Translated by Chris Turner. London: Verso, 2000.

———. *Open Sky*. Translated by Julie Rose. London: Verso, 1997. See esp. "Eye Lust."

———. *The Vision Machine*. Translated by Julie Rose. Bloomington, IN: Indiana University Press; London: British Film Institute, 1994.

Wiener, Norbert. *The Human Use of Human Beings: Cybernetics and Society*. New York: Da Capo, 1954.

Wilson, Ian. *The Shroud of Turin: The Burial Cloth of Jesus Christ?* Garden City, NY: Doubleday, 1978.

Wittgenstein, Ludwig. *On Certainty*. Edited by G.E.M. Anscombe. Translated by Denis Paul and G.E.M. Anscombe. New York: Harper Torchbooks, 1972.

Wollen, Peter. "Shooting Wars." *The Nation*, October 6, 2003.

Zielinski, Siegfried, Peter Weibel, and Daniel Irrgang, eds. *Flusseriana: An Intellectual Toolbox*. Minneapolis, MN: Univocal, 2015.

I would like to thank the John Simon Guggenheim Memorial Foundation for a fellowship that got this book started, and my graduate students over the past fifteen years, who helped me bring it into focus. And I would like to thank Lucas Zwirner and the team at David Zwirner Books, for believing in it.

DAVID LEVI STRAUSS is the author of *Co-illusion: Dispatches from the End of Communication* (2020), *Words Not Spent Today Buy Smaller Images Tomorrow: Essays on the Present and Future of Photography* (2014), *From Head to Hand: Art and the Manual* (2010), *Between the Eyes: Essays on Photography and Politics*, with an introduction by John Berger (2003; 2012), and *Between Dog & Wolf: Essays on Art and Politics in the Twilight of the Millennium* (1999; 2010). His text *In Case Something Different Happens in the Future: Joseph Beuys and 9/11* was published by documenta 13, in 2012. He is the editor of *To Dare Imagining: Rojava Revolution* (2016), with Dilar Dirik, Michael Taussig, and Peter Lamborn Wilson; and *The Critique of the Image Is the Defense of the Imagination* (2020), also with Taussig and Wilson. Strauss received the Infinity Award for Writing from the International Center of Photography in 2007 and a Guggenheim fellowship in 2003. He is the chair of the graduate program in Art Writing at the School of Visual Arts in New York.

"Ekphrasis" is traditionally defined as the literary representation of a work of visual art. One of the oldest forms of writing, it originated in ancient Greece, where it referred to the practice and skill of presenting artworks through vivid, highly detailed accounts. Today, "ekphrasis" is more openly interpreted as one art form, whether it be writing, visual art, music, or film, that is used to define and describe another art form, in order to bring to an audience the experiential and visceral impact of the subject.

The *ekphrasis* series from David Zwirner Books is dedicated to publishing rare, out-of-print, and newly commissioned texts as accessible paperback volumes. It is part of David Zwirner Books's ongoing effort to publish new and surprising pieces of writing on visual culture.

mother. The child has no conception at this point of what a mother or father is, but these words are forced upon him twenty-four hours a day. 'This is your mother.' Finally, the poor fellow says, 'She must be my mother,' but he does not have a clue as to what it means, even at the age of five. He is told to use the word 'mother', and so he just obeys and does so. We belong to God. He is the soul of our soul. You have not been able to understand this small point since eternity, and you have always considered yourselves to be the body and not the soul. As a result, you run after the objects of the senses, because your knowledge tells you that you must satisfy their hunger. You are incapable of thinking that it is the soul's hunger that must be appeased, because you do not accept that you are the soul and, therefore, a part of God. To accept that you are a part of God, an individual soul, is to accept the straightforward fact that:

The soul's hunger or thirst – its desire for form, sound, touch, and more – can only be fulfilled by its whole, and that whole is God.

ममैवांशो जीवलोके जीवभूत: सनातन:। (*Gita* 15.7)

The individual soul is an eternal part of God. This is not an imagined truth, something that is only applicable for a few days or in a single lifetime. This is an eternal truth. Ever since God has existed, so has this relationship. We just have to accept this one fact that He alone is ours. But you should not think, 'God alone is mine.' Instead, you should think, 'God is also mine.' When you go to a temple, you utter the verse, त्वमेव माता च पिता त्वमेव। What is the meaning of this verse? 'You alone are my father. You alone are my mother.'

The word 'alone', *eva*, is used. When you say alone, you cannot then accept anyone else as your mother. There is this condition of exclusiveness. However, because you love both God and this world, your relationship with Him has *also* mixed up in it. You say to Him, 'You are also mine, and the world is also mine.'

The condition specified by God in this regard is: 'I will assume your full responsibility when you accept only Me as yours.'

मामेकं शरणं व्रज। (*Gita* 18.66)

योगक्षेमं वहाम्यहम्॥ (*Gita* 9.22)

तेषामहं समुद्धर्ता। (*Gita* 12.7)

अहं त्वां सर्वपापेभ्यो मोक्षयिष्यामि। (*Gita* 18.66)

All these responsibilities that He assumes, such as preserving what you have, providing you with what you lack and protecting you from the results of sin, and so on, apply only to those who consider Him alone as theirs. This rule is not for those who have applied 'also' in their devotion.

Suppose a married woman in this world accepts another man as her husband and tells her actual husband, 'You are also my husband.' Her husband would say, 'What do you mean "also"?' She would answer, 'Yes, I have another husband,' to which he would reply, 'Then get out of my house!'

You do not have the courage to use 'also' even in worldly relationships, and this is a major illusory relationship between a man and a woman, simply strengthened by going seven times around a fire! But even here, you do not use 'also'. And with God you say, 'You are *also* mine,' because to say 'alone' implies ending attachments in the world, and you do not want to do that. Some people ask if they can keep their worldly attachments intact and attain God at the same time. This is impossible and can never happen because we attain what we have surrendered to. If you are attached mentally to the world, then you will attain the world. If your mind is attached to the Supreme Power, God, then you will attain Him.

यान्ति देवव्रता देवान्पितॄन्यान्ति पितृव्रताः।
भूतानि यान्ति भूतेज्या यान्ति मद्याजिनोऽपि माम्॥ (*Gita* 9.25)

This is clearly stated in the *Gita*: 'Whomsoever you love and are attached to in this life, after death you will attain their personality.'

Three sisters were married to three brothers who were all college graduates. The first brother was selected for the administrative services and went on to become a collector. The second brother could only become a clerk, and the third, falling into the company of drunkards and gamblers, could not get a job and became a beggar. Now how will the three sisters be addressed? The wife of the collector will be addressed as madam. The wife of the second brother will be called the clerk's wife, and the third brother's wife will be addressed as a female beggar. Although the three sisters have the same background, the same mother, they all are now in different situations.

Similarly, our mind is just like these girls. If the mind gets attached to somebody or something *tamasic*, you attain hell. If it finds some form of attachment with a *rajasic* person or thing, then you achieve the earthly region. If it is attached to a *sattvic* personality or thing, you attain celestial abodes, which are also temporary, like this material world. If the same mind is attached to the Supreme Power, you attain liberation and the bliss of divine love. It is that straightforward.

The condition is that our attachment should be exclusive. This exclusiveness can come about in one, two or even a thousand lifetimes, depending on your effort. You will have to practise incorporating this exclusiveness into your devotion, because you have repeatedly done nothing but tried to cheat others for your own selfish interests. Husband and wife, father and son, and master and servant spend twenty-four hours a day trying to exploit one another in order to satisfy personal self-interests. The person who is more adept at this act is more successful, but he can still never attain true peace or happiness. Even if an individual soul were to gain possession of infinite universes, this peace and happiness would still elude him.

The Restlessness

Thus, there is one knowledge that we have not acquired since beginningless time – each one of us is a soul and we have an eternal relationship with God alone. This world is meant for the maintenance of your body and not for your enjoyment. Simple food and a few clothes are all that you need. You should not desire more than this. Those who have their basic needs met are still unhappy. And those who are millionaires in this world are even more troubled!

Many people from affluent countries come running to India and roam its by-lanes looking for peace and happiness. Does it sell in the markets here? 'We have heard that these things can be attained in this country.' But you are millionaires, billionaires. 'Yes, but we cannot get a